J 388 .09 Laf

Lafferty, Peter.
Transport / Peter Lafferty. -- Oxford : Heinemann, 1992.
48 p. : ill. -- (Pioneers in science)

Includes index.
06827993 ISBN:0431007926

1. Transportation - History. I. Title

1319 93APR05 26/ 1-01010155

PIONEERS IN SCIENCE

TRANSPORT

PETER LAFFERTY

First published in 1992 by
Heinemann Children's Reference,
a division of Heinemann Educational Books Ltd,
Halley Court, Jordan Hill, Oxford OX2 8EJ

OXFORD LONDON EDINBURGH
MADRID PARIS ATHENS BOLOGNA
MELBOURNE SYDNEY AUKLAND SINGAPORE TOKYO
IBADAN NAIROBI GABORONE HARARE
PORTSMOUTH (NH)

Project manager Myra Murby
Editor Mary Melling
Designer Jerry Burman
Picture researchers Catherine Blackie, Suzanne Williams

Printed in Hong Kong

British Library Cataloguing in Publication Data

Lafferty, Peter
Transport. – (Pioneers in science)
1. Transport, history
I. Title II. Series
388.09

ISBN 0-431-00792-6

Photographic Acknowledgements

t=top b=bottom r=right l=left c=centre

Aviation Picture Library 39; Bridgeman Art Library 6, 9, 10t; Neil Bruce Photographic 26, 28t, 28b, 31bc; Dunlop 24; Mary Evans Picture Library 10b, 11, 14, 19, 21l, 32l, 32r, 33, 35l, 35r, 36; Heinemann Archive 16; Michael Holford 12 inset, 17b; Hulton Picture Company 13, 13t, 25; Mansell Collection 15; National Maritime Museum, Greenwich 17t; The National Motor Museum at Beaulieu 27, 29, 31bl, 31br; Peter Newark's Pictures 7, 20, 37, 38l; Novosti 41l; Popperfoto 18, 21r, 23r, 30; Rex Features 43t; Science Museum 8, 38r; Science Photo Library/NASA 40, 41r; Nigel Snowdon 43b; Taurus Graphics 4–5, 34, 39b; Zefa Picture Library 12, 22, 23t.

The photographs reproduced on pages 8 and 38r are reproduced by permission of the Trustees of the Science Museum.

Cover: Popperfoto l; Science Museum c; Novosti r; National Maritime Museum, Greenwich b.
Cover pictures show: Henry Ford l; Frank Whittle c; Valentina Tereshkova r; Painting of the Launching of the *Great Britain* in 1843 b.

Note to the reader
In this book there are some words in the text that are printed in bold type. This shows that the word is listed in the glossary on page 46. The glossary gives a brief explanation of words that may be new to you.

Contents

Introduction

Transport is crucial to our work and pleasure. Only 150 years ago it took months to go from Europe to Australia by ship and a day to travel less than 200 kilometres by coach and horse. Today, people can fly to Australia from Europe in 25 hours and **commuters** may travel 100 kilometres in an hour by train or car. In some large cities where there are a lot of people, cars and buses on the streets, it is possible to travel underground on trains.

Fast, efficient transport is an essential part of modern life. Whether we travel on public transport, such as trains and buses, or by private cars or bicycles, we are travelling in the inventions of pioneers in transport **science** and **technology**. Science is the study of the world and the way it works and technology is the way in which science can be used to make machines do useful tasks.

Cars, aircraft, railways, bicycles, motorcycles, ships and submarines all show how inventors have developed technology for modern travel. This book

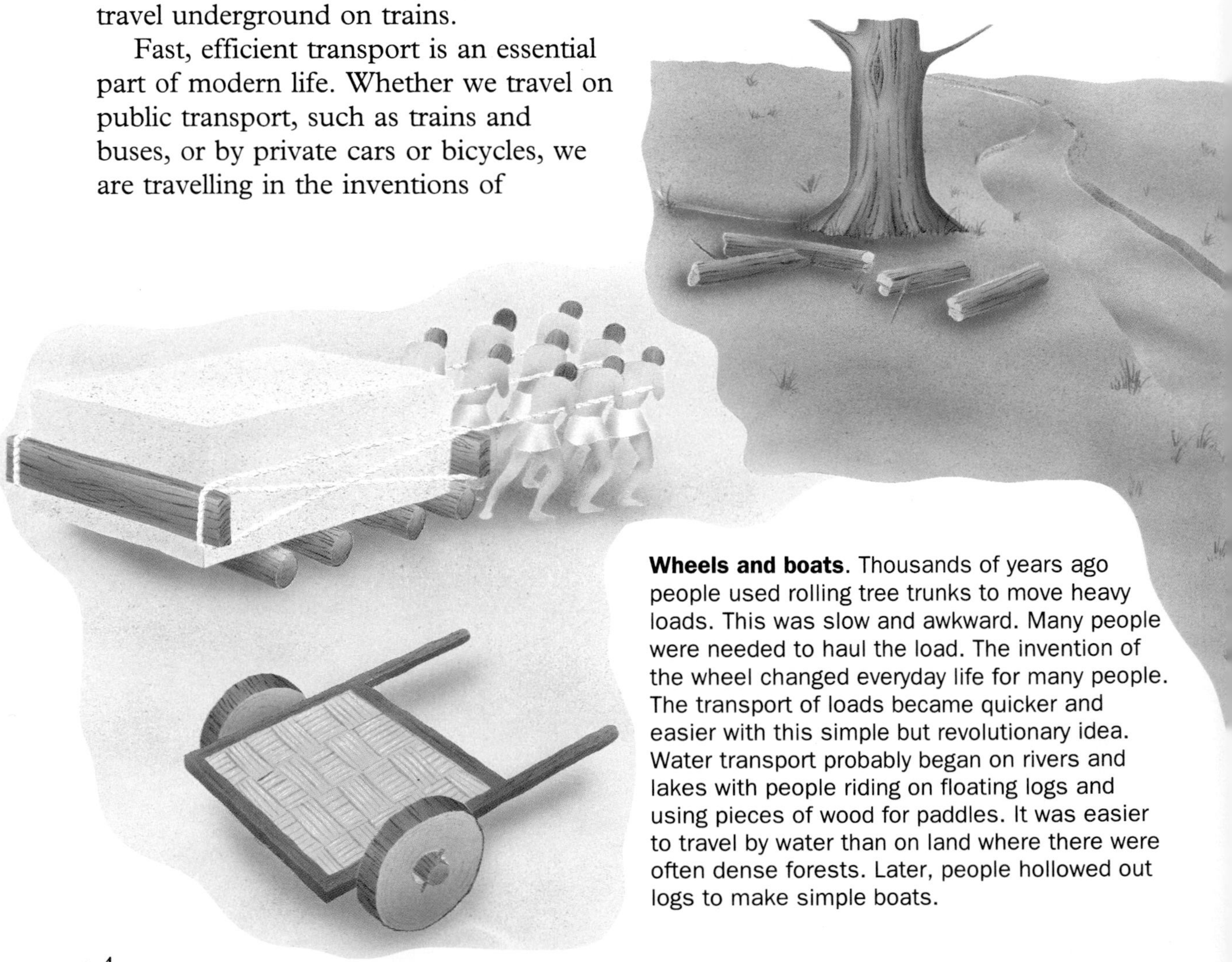

Wheels and boats. Thousands of years ago people used rolling tree trunks to move heavy loads. This was slow and awkward. Many people were needed to haul the load. The invention of the wheel changed everyday life for many people. The transport of loads became quicker and easier with this simple but revolutionary idea. Water transport probably began on rivers and lakes with people riding on floating logs and using pieces of wood for paddles. It was easier to travel by water than on land where there were often dense forests. Later, people hollowed out logs to make simple boats.

looks at the way these inventors and their transport inventions have changed people's lives through the ages.

Inventing the wheel

The wheel is one of the most important inventions of all time. You can see this by looking at the many objects around you that have wheels. Thousands of years ago, the ancient Egyptians used tree trunks as rollers to move heavy blocks of stone. This was very slow, because rollers had to be added at the front of the load as it was trundled along. The wheel was invented to speed up the process of moving large loads.

We do not know where the wheel was first used but the original wheels were probably circular slices cut from tree trunks. A thinner piece of wood, called an **axle**, joined the wheels as a crossbar.

The axle supported the load that was being moved. The first wheels were soon improved and their rims were covered with iron to help them last longer. About 4500 years ago, the Egyptians began to make lighter wheels. Instead of having solid wheels they used **spokes**, thin rods that join the rim of a wheel to the axle. This meant that carts were not so heavy and could move more quickly.

The first roads

Once wheels were being used it was possible to travel further and people needed good roads. The Romans built excellent roads about 2000 years ago because their soldiers and traders had to travel to countries far from Rome. The Romans made their roads from stone blocks. First they put a layer of stones in cement at the bottom. Then a layer of close-fitting stone blocks was put on top. The Romans also made strong stone bridges to carry the roads across valleys.

The first boat builders

Travel by water probably also started with the use of tree trunks. Perhaps someone climbed onto a log floating down a river. The flow of the river would have carried them along. The next stage was to hollow out a log to make a simple boat, called a **dugout**. A smaller piece of wood could have been used as a paddle to help them control their speed and direction. Before long, bigger and better boats were built by tying logs or bundles of reeds together.

Early days

During the years of the Roman Empire, travel between distant places was made easier because of the roads the Romans had built. By the year AD400, however, the Roman armies had left most of the countries they had occupied. Many of their roads were no longer repaired and these eventually became overgrown and full of potholes. Travel became difficult again and for many years, most people did not travel long distances on land. If they had to travel, they went on horseback, using narrow tracks and paths. Goods were carried by pack animals, such as horses and donkeys. In desert countries, camels were used as pack animals.

Early public transport

In towns, rich people sometimes travelled in a sedan chair. This was a chair that could be lifted and carried along by servants. The chair usually had a cover so that the person inside was protected from the weather. Only rich people could afford to be carried around in a sedan chair. Ordinary people had to walk.

Around 350 years ago, **carriages** were built to carry people. These were pulled by horses and were more comfortable to ride in. Coils of metal, called springs, were fitted underneath them to absorb the bumps and jolts caused by the rough roads.

The invention of the stage coach like this one leaving Biarritz in France was a very important development in transport. Travel was now possible for everyone, not just for people rich enough to have their own carriages. The coaches were usually drawn by four horses which would be changed many times during a long journey. Fresh horses were provided at inns along the route where there was also food and drink for the passengers. It was often a draughty and bumpy journey for the passengers who travelled on top of the coach as well as inside. Journeys which today only take a few hours by road or rail would take several days by stage coach.

Columbus landing at San Salvador, 1492. The development of ocean-going ships led to contact between different continents. Explorers who first discovered new continents planted their flags to show which country had discovered the new land.

About 1700, the first **stage coaches** were used. These took people from one town to another for a fare. The coach stopped at inns along the route to change the teams of horses. Stage coaches also carried the post. Until the railways were built, stage coaches were the main way of travelling on land in Europe and North America.

Making use of water

While roads were poor, goods were often carried by river or round coasts in boats and ships. By about 5000 years ago, the Egyptians had begun to build proper boats. Their first boats had been made from bundles of reeds. Later they learned to make stronger and bigger boats by joining together short planks of wood. They also invented the sail, which used the power of the wind to push their boats along. They fixed a paddle near the back of the boat to steer it.

The Vikings, who lived in northern Europe about 1000 years ago, also built fine boats. The Viking ships, called **longships**, were long and narrow. Each one had a large, square sail and some had as many as 80 oars. These ships carried the Vikings on voyages to Iceland, Greenland and America.

Discovering new lands

After the Vikings, even better boats were built. More masts and sails were added to give extra speed. A **rudder** was fixed to the back to steer the ship. Strong wood was used to make them safe in stormy seas.

These new ships allowed many explorers to make great voyages of discovery. In 1492 Christopher Columbus sailed from Spain and found the West Indies. In 1498 Vasco da Gama sailed round Africa to India. Ferdinand Magellan, setting out from Portugal in 1519, tried to sail right around the world. Although Magellan was killed during the journey, his crew sailed on to become the first people to sail completely round the world.

The coming of steam

The arrival of the steam **engine** in the 1700s brought big changes to people's lives. Before then, the only public transport was in coaches pulled by horses or in boats driven by sails and oars. The steam engine was the first powered machine to make things move. It was a very important invention because it meant that in future machinery and transport could be driven by a greater and more reliable source of power.

In a steam engine, water is heated in a boiler until steam is produced. The steam is fed into a hollow tube called a cylinder. Inside the cylinder, there is a **piston**. As the steam passes into the cylinder, the piston is pushed along and causes the machinery to turn.

The piston steam engine was invented by Thomas Newcomen. He was an ironmonger and blacksmith who was born in Devon, England. In 1712 Newcomen made a steam engine to pump water out of a coal mine near Dudley in the centre of England. The engine was huge. It was built in a building about 10 metres high. Poking through one wall was a long oak beam. The beam was connected to the piston of the engine. The piston was pushed up by steam from the boiler. Then a jet of cold water was squirted into the cylinder. This **condensed** the steam, turning it into drops of water. A **vacuum**, or airless space, was created in the cylinder. Air pressure then forced the piston down. Newcomen's invention made it safer for miners to dig deeper for coal because there was less fear of flooding in the mine.

The piston steam engine was a huge, noisy machine which saved the lives of many miners. It was invented by Thomas Newcomen in the early 1700s and was used to pump water from mines. This made it safer for the miners to dig deeper because there was less danger of flooding. On the right of the picture you can see the boiler where water was heated by a fire. Above the boiler is the tall cylinder where the expanding steam pushed the piston that moved the beam up and down.

This steam carriage first travelled from London to Bath in 1827. The 160 kilometre journey took more than nine hours. Steam carriages were not popular with everyone. Farmers were unhappy because their animals were frightened by the noise. There were also complaints that roads were being damaged by the weight of these heavy carriages.

Improved steam for factories

Fifty years later, Newcomen's engine was improved by James Watt. He was a mathematical instrument maker at Glasgow University in Scotland. In 1765 he was given a small Newcomen steam engine to repair. He realized that a great deal of heat was being wasted so he completely altered the engine, making it work more efficiently.

Watt's engine had a second, separate cylinder where the steam was condensed. This meant that the engine used much less fuel. It also produced more power because it did not rely on air pressure. Steam could now be used to move the piston both up and down. By 1782 his engine was working in many factories to turn cotton-spinning machines.

The first steam transport

Steam engines were also used on the road. In 1769 a Frenchman called Nicolas Cugnot built a three-wheeled steam wagon. It had a boiler at the front to make steam. This powered the front wheel. Unfortunately, Cugnot's wagon was difficult to steer. It also ran out of steam in about 12 minutes. On its first run, in Paris, it reached a speed of three kilometres an hour. Later, more successful steam road vehicles were built and by 1827 there was a steam carriage service between Bath and London.

The invention of the petrol engine in 1883 caused people to lose interest in steam-powered road vehicles. Petrol engines were smaller and cleaner than steam engines.

The first railways

The earliest railways were used in mines. Wagons full of coal were pulled along on wooden rails by horses. The tracks were smoother than a normal road, so a horse could haul more than twice as much coal as on a road. Unfortunately, the wooden tracks soon wore down. So, after a while, rails were made from iron or steel, a hard, strong metal made from iron. A British engineer, called Richard Trevithick, was the first to use a steam engine instead of a horse for rail haulage.

Pulling power

Richard Trevithick worked as an engineer in the mines of Cornwall and Wales. He built many steam engines for pumping water out of the mines. Then, in 1803, he built a steam engine, called a **locomotive**, to haul wagons along rails. In February 1804 the locomotive ran from Penydarren to Abercynon in South Wales. It hauled a 14-tonne train with 5 wagons and 70 men a distance of 15 kilometres at a speed of nearly 8 kilometres an hour. Unfortunately, the

◀ **Richard Trevithick**

◀ **The *Catch-Me-Who-Can***, built in 1808, was one of the first steam locomotives. It was given this name because it could travel at 20 kilometres an hour which was then thought to be very fast. It was designed by the British engineer Richard Trevithick who was an important pioneer of steam engines. The *Catch-Me-Who-Can* was used for pleasure rides on a small circular track near the present-day Euston station in London. Trevithick was a very clever engineer but not such a good businessman. He eventually died in poverty.

locomotive was so heavy that it broke the iron tracks in several places. So it was taken to pieces and was used to drive a hammer in an iron works instead.

In 1808 Trevithick built a locomotive to carry passengers. It was called *Catch-me-who-can*. This ran on a small circular track in London, near the site of the present-day Euston railway station. People paid a small amount for a ride. The train was great fun, and could travel at a speed of 20 kilometres per hours. However, it made little money for Trevithick.

Puffing Billy and *Wylam Dilly*

John Blenkinsop was the manager of a coal mine near Leeds, in England. He wanted to use steam engines to haul coal. In 1811 he designed a steam locomotive that used special rails. These had teeth built into one rail to stop the locomotive slipping as it went up slopes.

Another engineer, called William Hedley, improved Blenkinsop's design. He found that the teeth were only needed on steep slopes. So, he did away with the special rails. He also built more efficient steam engines. However, his engines were very heavy, and kept breaking the tracks. The answer was to increase the number of wheels on the locomotive. This spread the load and the tracks stayed in one piece.

Hedley built three locomotives. One of these was called *Puffing Billy*. It can be seen today in the Science Museum in London. The other engines were called *Wylam Dilly* and *Lady Mary*. The *Wylam Dilly* is now in the Edinburgh Museum in Scotland.

Puffing Billy was a steam locomotive built in 1813 by an engineer called William Hedley. It was used to pull coal trucks at the Wylam coal mine in north east England and replaced the horse-drawn trucks. *Puffing Billy* was far stronger than any horse and could pull bigger loads at a greater speed.

George Stephenson

When steam engines were first invented they were mostly used for working in coal mines. Steam engines were used to carry passengers along roads for a short time but they never became popular. The first person to develop proper passenger steam transport was George Stephenson. Instead of using the roads, he developed his engines to carry passengers along specially built rails.

Stephenson was born in 1781 in the village of Wylam in north east England. George was a clever boy, and taught himself to read and write by going to night school. He became interested in the steam engines like the *Puffing Billy* which were used to pump water out of the local coal mine. By 1812 he was put in charge of all the machinery used at the mine.

George was asked to build a locomotive for hauling coal. His first locomotive was called the *Blülcher* and ran in 1814. Over the next 12 years he built 16 other locomotives. In 1825 he made one to carry passengers. It was called *Locomotion*. Passengers were carried between Stockton and Darlington, a distance of 65 kilometres. On the trip *Locomotion* reached a speed of 24 kilometres an hour.

The Rocket

In 1829 Stephenson was asked to build another railway. This was to run from Liverpool to Manchester. A competition was held to find the best engine.

◀ **George Stephenson**

◀ **The *Rocket***, Stephenson's prize-winning locomotive, was built in 1829. All later steam engines developed from this early design.

Stephenson's entry was called the *Rocket*. It reached a speed of 46 kilometres an hour. This was faster than a horse could run. Some people thought that it might be impossible for travellers to breathe at these high speeds! The *Rocket* won first prize in the competition. After this success, George was asked to build other railways.

The railways spread fast. Lines were soon built from London to all the main towns in Britain. George Stephenson's son, Robert, helped in the work. He also became a famous engineer and built many railway bridges.

Around the world by rail

At first, many people in the rest of Europe were cautious about building railways. Many ordinary people were scared of trains. Then France and Germany bought locomotives made by Stephenson. The locomotive for the first German railway was called *Der Adler*, or the *Eagle*. In 1835 it arrived in Germany from England, complete with its driver, William Wilson. To impress the Germans, Wilson wore a top hat when he drove the train. He spent the rest of his life in Germany, driving trains. The first Russian railway also used a Stephenson locomotive. The railway opened in 1836 at St Petersburg, now called Leningrad.

Railways quickly spread to North America, where they became known as 'railroads'. One of the first passenger railroads in the United States ran from Charleston in South Carolina. In 1830, an engine called *The Best Friend of Charleston* made its first run. One day, the boiler blew up and the driver was killed. However, the locomotive was rebuilt and two years later the railroad was the longest in the world. Railroads were later built right across North America. They played an important part in opening up that vast continent.

Across the United States. The idea of railways soon spread from Britain to the rest of the world. In the 1860s in the United States there was a race between two companies to build a railway between the Atlantic and Pacific coasts. In 1869 it became possible to travel right across the United States by train. The picture shows a construction crew who worked on a new railway line in 1885.

The first steamships

Steam engines were first used to drive a ship in the early 1780s. In 1783 the Marquis de Jouffroy d'Abbans built a steamboat in France. Its steam engine turned **paddle wheels**, like the wheels of a water mill, to drive the ship along.

The first steamship service was started in 1790 by an American called John Fitch. His boat was called the *Experiment*. It had three large oars at the back. These were moved back and forth by a steam engine, and so pushed the boat along. The *Experiment* ran on the Delaware River in the eastern United States.

Riverboats

Robert Fulton was an American inventor who was famous for building bridges and ships. While living in France, he built a steamship. The ship was tested in 1803 on a journey down the River Seine. In 1806 Fulton went back to America, where the government helped him improve his ship.

In 1807 Fulton launched a new steamship. It was called the *Clermont*. This ship had two paddle wheels, one on each side of the **hull**, or body, of the ship. The *Clermont* steamed at about the same speed as a person could walk but it did not need to stop for a rest! It could carry about 100 people.

Steamships soon became popular. In America, the best way to travel long distances was by steamship along the rivers. Special steamships called **sternwheelers** were built. These had a large paddle wheel at the back, or **stern**.

One of the first steamships was the *Experiment*, designed by John Fitch. It worked like a rowing boat, with a steam engine to move the oars back and forth. The boat carried passengers on the Delaware River in the United States in 1790.

The *Sirius* was one of two paddle steamers to cross the Atlantic in a race in 1838. It took 18 days from Liverpool to New York. The other ship, the *Great Western*, took only 15 days.

Only a small part of the wheel went into the water, which meant that the sternwheelers could be used in shallow rivers.

An ocean race

Steamships sailed across the oceans too. At first they still had sails as well as engines. The sails were used if the engines broke down or if the ship ran out of **fuel**. Often so much fuel was needed that there was little room for cargo or passengers.

In 1838 there was a race across the Atlantic Ocean, from Liverpool to New York. Two steamships, the *Sirius* and the *Great Western*, took part. The *Sirius* had not been built to cross the Atlantic, and it ran out of coal. Cabin doors, furniture, planks and one mast were thrown into the firebox to keep the ship going. *Sirius* took 18 days to reach New York. The *Great Western*, which was the first steamship specially built to cross the Atlantic, did not run out of coal. It reached New York in just 15 days. The success of these steamships meant that people were now able to travel between Europe and the United States easily and quickly. This encouraged both trade and immigration and helped make the United States one of the largest and most powerful countries in the world.

Isambard Kingdom Brunel

Isambard Kingdom Brunel was a brilliant engineer who built bridges, railways and giant ships. He was born in Portsmouth, England, in 1806. One of his first jobs was to help his father, who was also a famous engineer, make a tunnel under the River Thames near London. This was the first tunnel ever built under that river.

Then Brunel began to build a railway from Bristol to London. This was opened in 1841 and was the finest railway in England. The trains could travel fast along the broad, straight tracks. Many of his bridges and tunnels are still used today. Another of his achievements was to design a bridge over a high gorge near Bristol, in the west of England. This is the famous Clifton Suspension Bridge.

A brilliant British engineer, Isambard Kingdom Brunel, was responsible for many of the improvements in transport that took place during his lifetime. His bridges, railways and ships made it possible to travel rapidly between cities and across oceans.

The giant ships

It was Brunel's dream to build giant ships. His first was called the *Great Western* and it was launched in 1838. It was 72 metres long, about twice the size of any other steamship, and had paddles driven by steam. The *Great Western* was the first steamship to provide a regular service across the Atlantic Ocean. It took just 15 days to make its first crossing. This was three days less than its rival, the *Sirius*.

In 1843 Brunel made an even bigger ship. It was called the *Great Britain* and was bigger than any ship built before. The *Great Britain* was made of iron, not wood, and helped show that iron ships were safe. It was the first ocean steamship to have a **propeller**, or a shaft fitted with blades, instead of paddles. Sadly, the *Great Britain* ran aground on its fifth voyage, and Brunel sold it. After many adventures, the *Great Britain* ran aground again near the Falkland Islands. However, in 1970, it was towed back to Britain and is berthed in Bristol harbour where it can now be visited.

The *Great Eastern*

Brunel's last ship was the biggest of all. It was launched in 1857 and was called the *Great Eastern*. The new ship was 210 metres long, over twice the length of the *Great Britain*. The *Great Eastern* was

The *Great Britain* was the first propeller-driven, iron, ocean-going steamer to cross the Atlantic. It was designed by Brunel and was launched in Bristol in 1843. *Great Britain's* first voyages were to America and then later it carried passengers to Australia. The *Great Britain* is now docked at Bristol and much of the ship has been restored for visitors to see.

◀ **The biggest ship built in the 19th century** was Brunel's last ship, *Great Eastern*. It was designed to carry 4000 passengers to Australia and India and was the only ship built with both paddle wheels and a screw propeller. The *Great Eastern* was too expensive to run and was not a success as a passenger liner but it became famous as the ship that laid the first successful transatlantic telegraph cable.

powered by both paddles and propellers, and had six masts for sails. It was designed to carry passengers to Australia and India and could carry enough coal for the round trip.

For over 40 years, the *Great Eastern* was the largest ship afloat. Unfortunately, it used a lot of fuel and was expensive to run so it was not a success as a passenger liner. Brunel was so worried by the huge cost of the *Great Eastern* that he became very ill, and he died in 1859. However, the *Great Eastern* did become famous as the ship that laid the first successful cable across the Atlantic Ocean in 1866. This cable made it possible to send cheap and swift telegraph messages across the ocean.

A better steam engine

Charles Parsons was a British engineer and inventor. He was born in 1854, the same year that his father, William Parsons, invented the 'iron-clad' or armour-plated warship. As a boy, Charles liked to make models and when he was older he studied engineering.

A new engine

Charles Parsons's first job was with a firm making steam engines for ships. This was at the time when passenger liners began racing across the Atlantic Ocean. Charles realized that the steam engines being used were at the limit of their power and could go no faster. If ships were to travel any faster, then a new type of engine was needed.

In 1884 Parsons designed an improved engine, called a **steam turbine**. In a steam turbine, a jet of steam flows through a set of spinning blades that turn as the steam passes through them. The first steam turbine engine was used to turn an electricity generator. In 1892 Parsons built a larger turbine that produced electricity for the city of Cambridge in England.

The Spithead sensation

Parsons then fitted one of his **turbine** engines into a small ship. It was called

A show of speed. To show how fast a turbine-powered ship could go, Charles Parsons disrupted a naval display at Spithead near Portsmouth in 1897. His boat the *Turbinia* sped between the Navy's ships at 60 kilometres an hour.

The first steam turbine liner. In November 1907 the *Mauritania* was the first steam turbine ship to cross the Atlantic. At the same time the ship won the Blue Riband, the prize awarded for the fastest Atlantic crossing without refuelling. Since then ship designers and captains have been competing to improve on the fastest speed and win the Blue Riband.

the *Turbinia*. The *Turbinia* was 30 metres long and had three propellers. The turbine engine almost filled the whole ship but it allowed the *Turbinia* to reach a speed of 60 kilometres an hour. This was faster than any other steamship at the time. Parsons tried to persuade the Royal Navy to use turbines in warships but they were not interested.

Parsons was determined to convince the Navy to use turbines and in 1897, in order to create a stir, he disrupted a naval display. The display was being held to celebrate the fiftieth anniversary of Queen Victoria's coronation. All the large ships of the Navy were assembled at Spithead, near Portsmouth, on the southern coast of England. During the ceremony, Parsons suddenly appeared in the *Turbinia*. He steered in and out of the warships at great speed. The *Turbinia* went so fast that it could not be caught and stopped. This created a sensation and the naval captains were convinced. They ordered that turbines should be fitted into warships and in 1905 Parsons's engine was fitted to the great ocean liners that sailed across the Atlantic Ocean.

Most modern steamships use turbines because they allow a ship to go faster than other steam engines. A type of turbine is also used today in the engines of large aircraft.

Under the waves

People have tried for hundreds of years to build ships that could travel under water. In 1578, an Englishman called William Bourne designed an underwater boat covered with waterproof leather but his boat was never built.

The first **submarine**, or underwater boat, to be built was made in 1620 by Cornelius van Drebbel, a Dutch inventor. His submarine followed Bourne's design and was made of greased leather stretched over a wooden frame with oars poking out through the sides. This strange boat was successfully used on the River Thames, near London, and King James I is said to have gone for a short ride in it.

The *Turtle* and the *Nautilus*

Another early submarine was used during the American Revolution. It was called the *Turtle*. It was built by a student called David Bushnell. The *Turtle* was built of wood and shaped like a walnut standing on end. When under water, the operator turned propellers at the rear to move the craft along.

Robert Fulton was another submarine pioneer. In 1800, while in France, he built a submarine called the *Nautilus*. This craft was made of copper sheets and it contained enough air to keep four people alive for three hours underwater. The *Nautilus* was also meant to be used to put explosives under enemy ships. At

The *Turtle* was an early submarine used during the American Revolution in 1776. It was built by a student called David Bushnell and was used in an unsuccessful attempt to blow up a British warship in New York Harbour.

The first modern submarine. The *Holland VI*, built by an American inventor, John Holland, in 1897, was the first submarine powered by an engine. It used a petrol engine on the surface and an electric motor when submerged. It could travel 800 kilometres on the surface and 40 kilometres under water.

that time France was at war with Britain. Fulton successfully sank an old ship in a test but when he set out to destroy British ships, he was too slow to catch those he sighted.

The modern submarine

The early submarines did not have proper engines. They could only be moved along when the crew turned the propellers by hand, which made them very slow. Different types of engines were tried. The *Plongeur*, a French submarine built in 1863, used an engine powered by **compressed air**.

In 1880, an English clergyman, George Garrett, made a submarine with a steam engine. The engine had to be turned off when the boat went under water or it would have used all the air. However, enough steam remained in the engine for short journeys. Electric motors were also tried but their batteries soon ran out of power.

It was an American inventor, John Holland, who finally found the answer in 1897. He built a submarine, called *Holland VI*, that used a petrol engine when on the surface, and an electric motor when submerged. This was the first modern submarine.

Nuclear-powered submarines can travel around the world without surfacing. *Nautilus*, built in 1955, was the first nuclear submarine. It travelled nearly 16 000 kilometres in its first year without needing to refuel.

Today's submarines are often **nuclear-powered**. The first nuclear submarine was called *Nautilus*, after Robert Fulton's craft. It was built in 1955. Nuclear-powered submarines are truly underwater ships. They can travel round the world without coming to the surface.

Skimming the waves

Even the fastest ships are slow compared with cars or aircraft. This is because they have to force their way through the water. Some types of modern craft have been built to skim across the water. One type is called the **hydrofoil**. This has small wings under its hull, which lift it out of the water as it moves along.

Flying through the water

The first hydrofoil was built in 1900 by an Italian called Enrico Forlanini. His boat had three sets of foils at the front and back and it reached a speed of 64 kilometres an hour. In 1911 Forlanini showed his hydrofoil to Alexander Graham Bell, the inventor of the telephone, on Lake Maggiore in northern Italy. In 1919 Bell used a hydrofoil boat on a lake in Canada, where it reached a speed of 100 kilometres an hour. Today, hydrofoils are used as ferries on lakes and rivers, and for short sea journeys.

Floating on air

Another type of craft that travels above the water is called the **hovercraft**. This floats on a cushion of air above the surface of the water. The hovercraft was invented by Christopher Cockerell, a British engineer who was born in 1910. During the Second World War, he worked for a radio company, developing **navigation** equipment to help bomber aircraft find their way. Later, he left to

A modern hydrofoil. As the boat speeds up, the hull lifts up out of the water. This means that the water does not slow the craft down. Today the largest hydrofoils weigh over 300 tonnes and still manage to reach speeds of over 90 kilometres an hour.

The hovercraft was invented by Christopher Cockerell in 1955. The modern hovercraft in this picture, which floats on a cushion of air above the surface of the water, carries passengers and cars between Britain and the continent of Europe. Other hovercraft are used for exploring rivers and for fighting harbour fires.

Christopher Cockerell (right) and chief test pilot, Peter Lamb, with a model of his hovercraft.

start his own boat hire business. It was while working with boats that he decided to build a boat that slid over the water as easily as a skate slides over ice. To do this he had to find some way to separate the hull of the boat from the water.

In 1955, Cockerell thought up the idea of using a strong downwards jet of air to hold the boat away from the water. He did many experiments using everyday objects like tin cans, kitchen scales, vacuum cleaners and hair driers. Large fans were used to suck in air and blow it downwards. He found that a strip of material, or **skirt**, was needed around the edge of the hull. This stopped too much air leaking out, and helped lift the craft out of the water. The craft was then driven forwards by large propellers mounted on the top.

When Cockerell told the Royal Navy about his invention, they were so impressed that they declared the invention 'Top Secret'! This stopped Cockerell from telling anyone else about it. However, eventually he was given permission to manufacture his new-style craft. The first hovercraft were made in 1959. Ten years later, giant hovercraft were being used to carry passengers and cars across the English Channel.

The bicycle boom

The first bicycles must have been very uncomfortable to ride. They were called 'dandy-horses' or 'hobby horses'. They had a wooden frame with a wooden wheel at each end. There was no proper seat, no pedals, and no way to steer! A rider had to move along by pushing on the ground, first with one foot and then with the other. These simple bicycles began to appear on the roads of France and Britain around 1790.

Gradually, improvements were made. In 1818 hobby horses were fitted with handlebars to help steering and then a simple saddle was fitted as a seat. However, they still had to be 'scooted' along with the feet.

The boneshakers

In 1839, a Scottish blacksmith, called Kirkpatrick Macmillan, made a hobby horse with pedals. The pedals were attached to the back wheel by rods. As the pedals were moved up and down, the back wheel turned around.

In about 1861, a Frenchman named Ernest Michaux had the idea of fitting the pedals to the front wheel. This was easier for the rider, and simpler to make. Michaux then made the front wheel larger than the back wheel. This made it possible to go faster. Michaux bicycles were known as boneshakers because they were still uncomfortable to ride. However, improved designs made from steel and with hard rubber tyres soon appeared.

The penny-farthing

James Starley of Coventry, England, was called 'the father of the cycle industry'. In 1870 he introduced the 'penny-farthing' bicycle. This bicycle was very popular, but riders were often insulted or attacked by other road users. In 1876, a British coachman was fined for whipping a cyclist who was overtaking him. The guard on the coach was also fined for hurling an iron ball at the cyclist!

The penny-farthing was difficult to ride. If a penny-farthing stopped suddenly, the rider would be thrown over the handlebars onto the ground.

John Dunlop, a Scottish veterinary surgeon living in Belfast in 1888, invented the tyres that we still use today. It was his idea to make a tyre filled with air, known as pneumatic tyres. This gave a much more comfortable ride than the earlier tyres that were made of solid rubber.

A penny-farthing race in New York in 1890. The penny-farthing was one of the early bicycles and was so called because it had a very large front wheel and a very small back wheel. At that time the penny was the largest British coin and the farthing was the smallest. The penny-farthing was difficult to ride and needed a push from behind to get started.

The safety bicycle

The first 'safety bicycle' was made by Harry Lawson and ridden around the streets of Brighton, England, in 1873. The two wheels on a safety bicycle were the same size. The pedals were connected to the back wheel by a chain and the brake was attached to the back wheel. These features meant that the safety bicycle was easy and safe to ride.

The final improvement to the bicycle was the invention of the air-filled rubber tyre. John Boyd Dunlop, a Scotsman, invented these tyres in 1888. Within a few years, all bicycles were fitted with them. They made a bicycle ride smooth and comfortable.

Motorcycle power

The earliest motorcycles were simple bicycles driven by small steam engines. It is thought that one of these steam bicycles was ridden in Paris as early as 1818. Steam-driven tricycles with three wheels were probably used in 1831. In 1868 Ernest and Pierre Michaux attached a small steam engine behind the saddle of one of their velocipedes, or boneshaker bicycles. The engine was connected to the back wheel by leather belts. Like other steam-driven bicycles, the Michaux machine could not go very fast. The steam engine was too heavy and did not have enough power.

The petrol engine

Over the years, there had been many attempts to make a light and powerful engine. The earliest design for such an engine was made in 1678 by a Dutch scientist, Christian Huygens. He suggested using gunpowder as a fuel, or source of power. Other early engines used gas as a fuel. These engines burned, or exploded, a fuel inside the engine to produce power. They are called **internal combustion engines**.

The modern internal combustion engine was invented by a German engineer, Nikolaus Otto, in 1876. Otto's engine used gas or oil as the fuel. In 1883, his former assistant, Gottlieb Daimler, discovered how to use petrol as a fuel instead. Petrol is a more powerful fuel than gas or oil, so Daimler's improved engine was more powerful than earlier ones.

Daimler fitted the engine to a wooden

Gottlieb Daimler built the first motorcycle with a petrol engine in 1885. Daimler made this motorcycle by attaching a petrol engine to a modern bicycle frame. The motorcycles we know today look very different from this one, but they still have petrol engines.

A motorcycle trip in 1914. The passenger rides in a sidecar that could be attached to the motorcycle to carry passengers. People had to wrap up well to protect themselves from dust and bad weather.

bicycle to make a motorcycle. The cycle was built and ridden by his partner, Wilhelm Maybach, in 1885. After the first test run, the local newspaper attacked Daimler. It called his motorcycle 'diabolical and dangerous to the life and well-being of the citizens', and suggested that the police take drastic action!

The modern motorcycle

Motorcycles that we would recognize were not made until much later. There were a number of different designs, with the engine attached to the frame in different ways. The best design had the engine attached to the frame of a safety bicycle. The Hildebrand and Wolfmuller factory in Germany went into production making such bikes in 1894.

However, it was the two Werner brothers who introduced the modern design in France in 1901. They made motorcycles with the engine at the bottom, where the pedals are on a pedal cycle. They introduced other improvements, too. The engine was controlled by grips on the handlebars. Since then, almost all motorcycles have followed their basic design.

The first cars

One of the most important inventions in the history of transport is the motor car. This allowed ordinary people to have their own private form of powered transport. The car industry was founded just over a hundred years ago by two German engineers, Gottlieb Daimler and Karl Benz.

Gottlieb Daimler's first car was made in 1885. Here Daimler is sitting in the back and his son is in front.

The horseless carriage

Gottlieb Daimler was born in 1834, the son of a baker in the town of Schorndorf in Germany. Young Gottlieb was always interested in machines and became a skilled engineer. In 1885 he fitted a petrol engine to a carriage that was normally drawn by a horse to make the first car. It was called a 'horseless carriage'. It had four wheels and could carry four people. Daimler went on improving his engine over the next few years.

The car-maker

Karl Benz was born in Karlsruhe, Germany, in 1845. As a boy, he was

Karl Benz's first car was made in 1885. It looked like a tricycle, with a frame made of steel tubes and wire wheels. It had trouble going up hills and could only travel at 12 kilometres an hour.

interested in all mechanical things, and learnt to repair clocks. He made his first car at about the same time as Daimler, in 1886. The Benz car was lighter than Daimler's and could only carry the driver and one passenger.

The first trials of the Benz car were not encouraging. The car either refused to start, or started so suddenly that the passengers were thrown out! Eventually the car was persuaded to make a non-stop run of just under a kilometre, at a speed of 12 kilometres an hour. Despite this success, the local newspaper called the car 'useless, ridiculous and indecent'!

It was Karl's wife Bertha who showed how useful her husband's invention could be. In the summer of 1888, she took one of the cars without Karl's permission and set out to visit relatives. At every village they passed through, they startled people and horses. The car had to be pushed up hills. In one village, a cobbler had to repair the brakes. At another village, a hatpin was used to unblock a pipe carrying petrol to the engine. Another time, an elastic garter was used to make a repair. The journey, which today would take less than an hour, took all day. Nevertheless, Bertha had proved her point. A new means of transport had been born.

Benz was the first person to make cars for sale. He started a factory in 1894. Unlike Daimler, he did not keep improving his design and he kept the same one for over 15 years. By the time he died in 1929, the motor car had become a common sight on roads all around the world.

Motoring in the 1890s could be quite uncomfortable. The driver and passengers were exposed to dust and bad weather. Until 1896, in Britain, a man with a red flag had to walk in front of all motor vehicles to warn pedestrians.

Cheaper motoring

Only rich people could afford to buy one of the early cars. Henry Ford was the person who first made cheap motor cars. In 1896 he built his first car in his spare time, in a garden shed. Seven years later, Henry Ford started his own company to make cars. Today the Ford Motor Company is one of the biggest makers of cars in the world.

Cars for everyone

Henry Ford was born in 1863 in Dearborn, Michigan, in the United States of America. In 1902 he set up the Ford Motor Company in Detroit. At that time, motor cars were still expensive. Ford's aim was to make a speedy and reliable car, at a low price.

Ford started making cars in a new way. He split the work of building a car into a number of different jobs and each worker in his factory did just one job. Ford put moving **conveyor belts** in his factories. These slow-moving belts carried the cars and as the cars moved along each worker did his job on the car. At the end of the conveyor belt, the cars were finished. This way of working was faster than the old methods of building cars one at a time. It was called **mass production**.

The Tin Lizzie

The first cheap, reliable car was built in 1908. It was called the Model T, and nicknamed 'Tin Lizzie'. A Model T could be made in just 90 minutes in the Ford factory. Factories using old methods took 12 hours to make a car.

From Model T to Mini

Mass production meant that cars became cheaper and many more people could afford them.

The most popular car ever made was the Volkswagen 'Beetle'. This was designed by Ferdinand Porsche in 1938 and went into production in 1945. It was made for over 40 years, the longest manufacturing life-time of any car. Over 21 million 'Beetles' were made. In 1977 one new 'Beetle' was being produced every 14 seconds.

The best-selling British car was the

The pioneer of cheap motoring, Henry Ford, driving his first car, called the 'Quadricycle', which he designed in 1896.

The production line. Workers at this Ford factory in 1913 are involved in the final stage of assembling a Model T Ford. One by one, the almost-completed cars are wheeled forward to have their seats and bodywork attached. Using this method increased the speed of car production.

Mini, which was designed by Alec Issigonis. Over 5 million Minis have been sold since 1959. Despite its small size, a Mini can carry four people because its engine is fitted in a new way. Instead of fitting lengthways into the engine compartment, Issigonis designed it to fit sideways. This leaves more room for passengers.

The mass production of cheap cars has meant that more people are able to travel independently. However, this has also caused problems. More cars mean more **air pollution** and more roads. If we build more roads, we have to destroy a great deal of countryside.

Twentieth-century best sellers. Small, cheap cars like the French Citroen 2CV, the German Volkswagen Beetle and the British Mini have allowed millions of people to enjoy the advantages of owning a car.

Pioneers of flight

The first successful flying machines were balloons filled with hot air. Hot air is less **dense** than cold air. This means that a balloon filled with hot air rises. A hot air balloon was sent up on 15 June 1783 by two French brothers called Joseph and Etienne Montgolfier. They made a balloon measuring about 10 metres across out of linen and paper. An opening at the bottom was held over a fire of straw and rags. The balloon soon filled with smoke and hot air and when released it rose to a height of about 1800 metres.

In September 1783, they showed their balloon to the King and Queen of France. The balloon carried a sheep, a cockerel and a duck. After a short flight, the animals landed safely. On 21 November 1783, the first human passengers were carried up in a balloon. The flight lasted 25 minutes and covered a distance of nine kilometres.

▲ **Ballooning pioneers**, Joseph and Etienne Montgolfier.

◀ **The Montgolfier balloon** takes off from outside the royal palace of Versailles in France, in September 1783. The Montgolfier brothers sent up three animals to see whether there was enough air, high up, for them to breathe. The animals survived, and this encouraged the brothers to send two men up in November 1783.

Otto Lilienthal gliding off a hill. Lilienthal's gliders could be more closely controlled by the pilot. He controlled the glider partly by swinging his legs. However, in 1896 a gust of wind took him out of control and he crashed to his death, about a year after this photograph was taken.

High adventure

The first flight across the English Channel was made in 1785 by the American John Jeffries and the Frenchman Jean-Pierre Blanchard. The flight was very nearly a disaster. The balloon leaked badly. To keep airborne, the two pilots were forced to throw overboard everything they could think of. Blanchard even threw out his trousers! This saved the day and they landed safely in a forest near Calais, wearing only their underpants. They had with them only a bottle of brandy and the first 'air mail' letters.

The trouble with balloons was that they were slow and they were easily blown around by strong winds. So inventors looked for other ways of flying.

The first aeroplane

It was Sir George Cayley who designed the first flying machine, with wings and a tail like those flying today. Sir George was a wealthy Englishman who was born in 1773. He made **gliders**. These are flying machines without engines. In 1849 he built a glider with three sets of wings. This was launched from a hillside with a ten-year-old boy on it but it only stayed in the air for a few seconds.Despite this, Sir George designed other gliders.

A German engineer called Otto Lilienthal had greater success with his gliders. He designed the first gliders to be controlled by the pilot. In the 1890s he made several flights but finally crashed and was killed in 1896.

The flying brothers

The Wright brothers, Orville and Wilbur, invented and built the first powered aircraft to take off and land safely.

Early attempts

Orville and Wilbur Wright lived most of their lives in Dayton, Ohio, in the United States of America. They became interested in the gliders that some inventors were beginning to fly, and in 1899, they made their own small glider. It was flown like a passenger-carrying kite, at the end of a line. They gradually progressed, making better gliders as they learned more. They invented a way of controlling the glider by twisting the wing tips. Before that, pilots controlled gliders by changing the position of their bodies. They had to test over 200 different types of wing before they eventually made a successful glider in 1902.

The next step was to put an engine in the glider. As there were no suitable engines available, the Wright brothers made their own. Then they experimented with propellers designed to pull the craft through the air. After months of work, their aircraft was ready. It had two propellers driven by a chain from the engine.

The air age begins

The Wrights' historic first flight took place on a freezing cold morning on 17 December 1903 at Kitty Hawk, in North Carolina. With Orville at the controls, their craft remained in the air for just over 12 seconds. It flew a distance of 36 metres. Later in the day they made longer flights. Their machine, called *Flyer*, was only 6.5 metres long, and could carry only one person.

During 1904 and 1905, the Wright brothers made more than a hundred flights, using a second aircraft. In 1906 they made a flight lasting an hour. Two years later they gave demonstrations in France, which convinced most people that the air age had really arrived.

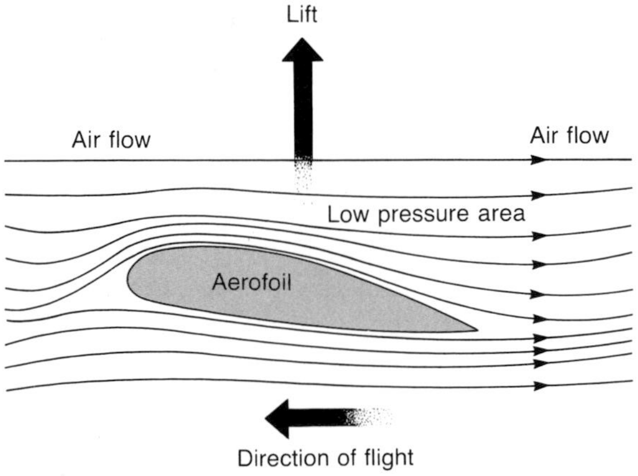

Getting airborne. The cross section of an aircraft wing (or helicopter blade) has a special shape called an aerofoil. It is rounded on the top, and flat on the bottom. As the aircraft accelerates down the runway, the air passing over the top of the wing travels faster over the rounded surface than the air passing underneath. A low pressure area is created on the top and the wing is drawn upwards. This produces lift.

▲ **Wilbur and Orville Wright**

▶ **The Wright brothers' *Flyer*** was the first aircraft to fly with an engine. Orville Wright flew the aircraft for the first time at Kitty Hawk in the United States in 1903. The pilot lay across the wing, holding on to a bar in front to stop himself from falling.

Hopping across the oceans

Other brave men also built aircraft and made long flights to prove that aircraft were safe. In 1909, a Frenchman called Louis Blériot flew over the English Channel. Then, in 1919, John Alcock and Arthur Brown became the first people to fly non-stop across the Atlantic Ocean.

The pioneering work of the Wright brothers opened a door onto the world. In the years after their discovery, the aircraft was developed into a larger and more powerful machine that could carry many people all over the world.

The helicopter story

The first **helicopter** was designed in 1483 but it never flew. Leonardo da Vinci, the famous Italian artist and scientist, designed a flying machine with a screw or spiral-shaped wing that turned round to lift the machine into the air. He called the machine *helix pteron*, which is Greek for 'spiral wing'. This is where our word helicopter comes from.

Leonardo's machine would not have worked if it had been built. Although the rotating wing would have lifted the machine, if a powerful enough engine had been used, it would have spun and wobbled in the air and then crashed.

Lift off

The first helicopters only managed to get off the ground after the development of powerful petrol engines in about 1900. However, these helicopters were unsteady and pilots refused to test fly them unless the machines were tethered to the ground. The first successful lift off took place on 13 November 1907 in a helicopter designed by a French inventor called Paul Cornu. It rose straight up to a height of 1.5 metres and hovered for about 20 seconds.

In 1923 a Spanish inventor, Juan de la Cierva, made a strange machine. It had

The first helicopter flight. Paul Cornu's strange-looking machine took off in 1907 and rose 1.5 metres in the air. It had to be attached to the ground by a safety rope because it spun and wobbled in the air.

The VS-300, the first practical helicopter, was built by Igor Sikorsky in 1939. This design, with a single rotor and tail control, became the pattern for modern helicopters.

wings and a propeller like an ordinary aeroplane. However, on top, it had blades that could rotate. It was called the windmill plane, or **autogiro**. As the autogiro flew, the top blades turned. This gave the plane extra lift. Because of this, it could fly slowly and take off safely from a short runway.

Modern helicopters

The first helicopter to work properly was made by Heinrich Focke in Germany in 1936. Focke's helicopter had two rotating blades that turned in opposite directions. This meant that the helicopter did not spin in the air.

In about 1939, an American called Igor Sikorsky also made a successful helicopter. Sikorsky attached a small propeller to the tail of his helicopter. This small **rotor** kept the craft from spinning in the air. Sikorsky had to design a way of tilting the rotating blades to make the helicopter move forwards. At one time, his helicopter could fly in every direction except forwards! By 1941, the problems had been overcome helicopters were produced for use in the Second World War.

The invention of the helicopter has made it possible for people to travel by air to places that conventional aircraft cannot reach. This is because helicopters can hover in the air and they do not need a runway to take off or land. Helicopters are also often used to rescue people from the sea, mountains, or road accidents.

Faster, higher

The **jet engine** was a very important invention in the history of air travel. Jet engines are powerful and efficient, making it possible for aircraft to carry many passengers at high speeds on long journeys.

Jet engines use a fuel such as kerosene, which is burned in a combustion chamber. The hot gases escaping from the combustion chamber pass from the rear of the engine, pushing the engine forwards. As the gases pass out of the engine, they go through a turbine, causing its blades to turn. The blades of the turbine are attached to a shaft. The **shaft** is connected to another turbine-like device, called a **compressor**, at the front of the engine. As the compressor is turned by the turbine, the air needed to burn the fuel is drawn into the engine at the front. The compressor squashes, or compresses, the air and forces it at high pressure into the **combustion chamber** where it burns fiercely.

The two inventors

The jet engine was developed at almost the same time by two engineers, one British and one German. In 1937 an English engineer called Frank Whittle built the first successful jet engine in an

Frank Whittle

Whittle's first jet aircraft. Frank Whittle built the first working jet engine in 1937. In 1941 his engine was used for the first time in the Gloster E28/39 aircraft. In 1939, while Whittle was developing his engine, von Ohain sent the first jet engine into the air.

old factory in Rugby, England. The engine did not run well. It leaked fuel and often caught fire. Once it ran at too high a speed and blew up.It was not until 15 May 1941 that Whittle's engine flew. It was mounted in a tiny aircraft, called the E28/39, built by the Gloster Aircraft Company. The E28/39 reached a speed of 560 kilometres an hour on its test flight.

Meanwhile, unknown to Whittle, a German called Hans von Ohain was also building a jet engine. Although Whittle's engine was the first to run, von Ohain's engine was the first into the air. On 24 August 1939 the engine was used to power a Heinkel 178 aircraft.

Faster than sound

The invention of the jet engine meant that aircraft would eventually travel faster than sound — that is more than one kilometre in three seconds. The first

Faster than sound. The Bell X-1 was the first aircraft to travel faster than sound, in 1947.

aircraft to do this was the rocket-powered Bell X-1 in 1947. This American aircraft, piloted by Charles 'Chuck' Yeager, reached a speed of 1078 kilometres an hour at a height of 2800 metres over California. Two years later, the first jet airliner — the British de Havilland Comet — took off. The Comet made its first flight with fare-paying passengers in 1952. Since then, millions of people have flown abroad in jet aircraft on holiday or to go to business meetings.

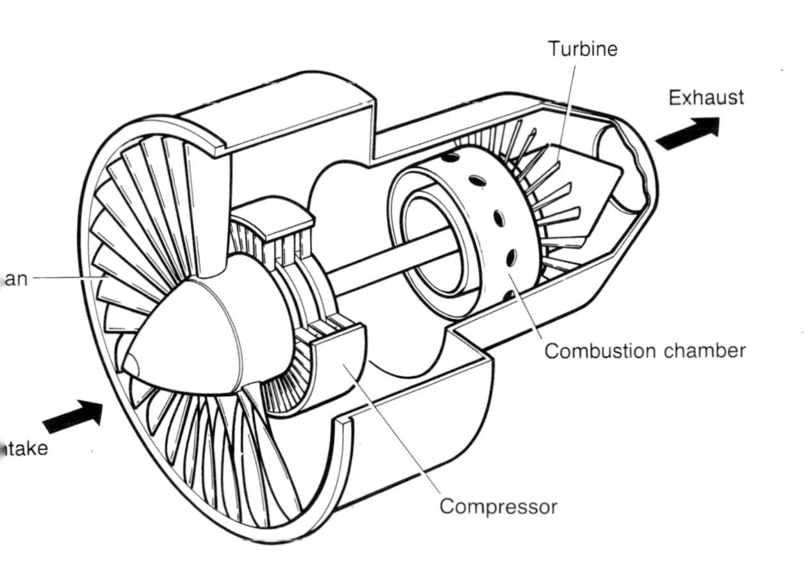

In a jet engine air is drawn in by a fan. The air is compressed and then it goes into the combustion chambers. There it burns with the fuel. Very hot gases are produced. These gases expand and escape out of the exhaust at the back. As the gases rush at great speed through the engine they do two things. The force of the gases pushes the engine, and the aircraft, forward. Also the gases turn the blades of a turbine. This rotates, driving the fan and the compressor. In this way more air is sucked into the front of the engine.

Into space

As early as AD180 a Greek writer called Lucian described an imaginary journey to the Moon. However, it was not until the 1890s that people began to look seriously at the possibility of travelling into space. By this time, scientists had begun to develop powerful fuels and inventors were starting to produce machines that were capable of travelling above the ground.

A Russian teacher named Konstantin Tsiolkovsky thought a **rocket** could be used. Rockets are tubes containing fuel. When the fuels burn rapidly, gases escape from the base of the tube, pushing it forwards or upwards with great force. Tsiolkovsky realized that only a rocket could provide the enormous force, or thrust, needed to lift people into space. Tsiolkovsky never built a rocket, but many scientists followed his ideas.

It was not until 1926 that an American, Robert H. Goddard launched the first successful liquid-fuelled rockets. During the Second World War, the Germans designed even better rockets, using Goddard's ideas. These ideas were later used by the Russians and Americans to build rockets for spaceflight.

The first man in space

On 12 April 1961 a Russian pilot named Yuri Gagarin became the first person in space. His ball-shaped spacecraft, called *Vostok 1*, was only 290 centimetres in diameter. Launched by a rocket, it reached a height of 327 kilometres. It

The first liquid-fuel rocket. Robert Goddard built this small rocket in 1926. It rose only a few metres from the ground, but inspired people to build better rockets. In later years, Goddard's ideas were used to send people into space.

took 89 minutes to circle or orbit the Earth once, travelling at nearly 28 000 kilometres an hour. Gagarin's flight lasted just 108 minutes.

Men on the Moon

On 21 July 1969, an American called Neil Armstrong became the first person to set foot on the Moon. Watched by 500 million television viewers worldwide, Armstrong climbed down the ladder of his small spacecraft, called the lunar module, and walked on the surface of the Moon. Later, Edwin 'Buzz' Aldrin joined Armstrong. They spent two and a half hours doing experiments and collecting rocks. Then they returned to the lunar module and blasted off to rejoin the third astronaut, Michael Collins, who had been circling the Moon in the main spacecraft called the command module.

Space travellers

Since then, the Soviet Union and the United States of America have sent many people into space. The first woman in space was a Russian called Valentina Tereshkova. In June 1963 she spent nearly three days orbiting the Earth. The longest space flight was made by Musa Manarov and Vladimir Titov of the Soviet Union. They spent 365 days in the Mir space station circling the Earth before returning on 21 December 1988.

The further we go into space, the more we can learn about the Universe. In 1976 two **robot probes** called *Viking* landed on Mars. They showed us that the surface of Mars is a red, stony desert where there is no life. Probes have now visited all the planets, except for the most distant one, Pluto. Four spacecraft, *Pioneers 10* and *11* and *Voyagers 1* and *2*, are now leaving our planetary system. All four are expected to continue travelling for several million years. *Pioneer 10* had a head start on the other three but it and *Pioneer 11* will be overtaken by the two *Voyagers*. By early 1990, *Pioneer 10* was over 7000 million kilometres from the Sun.

The first woman in space was a Russian called Valentina Tereshkova. In June 1963, she spent three days in space. It was not until the 1970s, when the space stations were developed, that people could stay for a longer time in space.

The first moon walk. In July 1969, Edwin 'Buzz' Aldrin stepped onto the Moon a few minutes after Neil Armstrong. There were more journeys to the Moon after this expedition, but the last one was in 1972. Journeys to the Moon are very expensive, and scientists are now working on different ways of travelling into space.

Transport of the future

Many of the methods of transport invented over the years have harmed the world around us and one of the main challenges facing scientists today is to make engines that are safer, cleaner and less wasteful of fuel.

Magnetic trains

The railway of the future may use **magnetic levitation**, which means 'raising by magnets'. These 'Maglev' trains will have no wheels. They will be held a short distance above the track by magnets. These trains will be very fast, but the special track will be costly to build. An experimental passenger train using magnets has already been built in Japan. It can travel at over 400 kilometres an hour.

New ways of flying

Some aircraft of the future may be strange-looking craft with forward-swept wings. This design makes the craft very manoeuvrable at high speeds, but computers are needed to help the pilot. New light aircraft may even be human-powered.

In 1988 a Greek called Kanellos Kanellopoulos, flew from Crete to the island of Santorini, 118 kilometres away, entirely under his own power. There was no motor in his aircraft, which was an extra-light flying machine called *Daedalus*. It was named after a legendary inventor from ancient Crete who tried to fly.

The strange-looking craft used by Kanellopoulos was made of strong and light carbon fibres and thin plastic sheeting. It had wings 35 metres across. The pilot, sitting in the cabin, pedalled to turn a large propeller at the front. The aircraft was slow moving and it only reached a speed of 29 kilometres an hour, and flew at a height of only five metres.

Power from the Sun

The car of the future may use **solar power**. It will get its power from the Sun. The solar-powered car would not make smelly fumes that would pollute the air. These cars are already with us. In 1990 strange vehicles could be seen racing across the desert of Australia. On the top of the cars were **solar cells**, which turned the Sun's energy into electricity. The electricity turned the wheels of the car.

The winner of the race was a car called *Spirit of Biel*. It resembled a giant pink and blue cockroach. It was very expensive to make, yet it could only manage an average speed of 70 kilometres an hour. Even so, it travelled from Darwin in the north of Australia to Adelaide in the south, a distance of 3138 kilometres, in six days.

Solar-powered aircraft have been developed, too. A solar-powered aircraft called the *Solar Challenger* flew across the

Solar power is an important development because it does not waste fossil fuels and does not pollute the atmosphere. The *Spirit of Biel* won a race for solar-powered cars across Australia in 1990. The aircraft *Solar Challenger* also gets power from the sun. Here it is shown flying across the English Channel in 1981. However, solar power is still expensive because many solar cells have to be used to produce enough electricity to power a car or aircraft.

English Channel in 1981. The 262-kilometre flight from Paris to Kent took over five hours.

Solar power has been used for a long time in spacecraft. Most craft exploring the distant planets are powered by solar cells. Unfortunately, solar power is still too expensive to be used in ordinary cars or aircraft. However, scientists are working to make cheaper solar cells. Perhaps one day prices will come down. Then we will have transport that does not cause **air pollution** nor waste the Earth's resources.

Time chart

Date	Pioneers	Achievement
4000-3000BC	The Egyptians	Use sailing boats on the Nile
3200BC	The Babylonians	Use the simple wheel at Ur, in Iraq
2500BC	The Egyptians	Use spoked wheels
1483	Leonardo da Vinci	Designs a simple helicopter
1578	William Bourne	Designs the first submarine
1620	Cornelius van Drebbel	Builds the first submarine on the River Thames
1712	Thomas Newcomen	Builds the first powerful steam engine
1765	James Watt	Improves the steam engine
1769	Nicolas Cugnot	Makes the first steam-driven road vehicle
1776	David Bushnell	Builds the submarine Turtle
1783	Marquis de Jouffroy	Sails the first steam boat on River Seine, in France
1783	Joseph and Etienne Montgolfier	Fly the first hot-air balloon
1785	John Jeffries and Jean-Pierre Blanchard	Make the first balloon flight across the English Channel
1790	John Fitch	Operates the first steamship service
1800	Robert Fulton	Builds the submarine Nautilus
1802	Richard Trevithick	Builds the first locomotive
1807	Robert Fulton	Builds the steamship Clermont
1825	George Stephenson	Starts the first railway service
1829	George Stephenson	The Rocket wins a competition
1830		The first railroad in America
1835	William Wilson	The first engine-driver in Germany
1838		The first race across the Atlantic by the Sirius and the Great Western
1839	Kirkpatrick Macmillan	Builds the first bicycle
1841	Isambard Kingdom Brunel	Opens a railway from London to Bristol
1843	Isambard Kingdom Brunel	Builds the Great Britain
1849	George Cayley	Experiments with gliders
1857	Isambard Kingdom Brunel	Launches the Great Eastern
1861	Ernest Michaux	Invents bicycle pedals
1869	Ernest and Pierre Michaux	Build a steam-driven motor cycle

Date	Pioneers	Achievement
1870	James Starley	Introduces the 'penny-farthing' bicycle
1873	Harry Lawson	Builds a safety bicycle
1876	Nikolaus Otto	Builds an oil or gas-fuelled internal combustion engine
1880	George Garrett	Builds a submarine with a steam engine
1883	Gottlieb Daimler	Builds first petrol engine
1884	Chales Parsons	Builds the first steam turbine
1885	Gottlieb Daimler	Builds the first motorcycle with a petrol engine
1885	Karl Benz and Gottlieb Daimler	Build the first petrol-driven motor cars
1888	John Dunlop	Invents the air-filled tyre
1897	John Holland	Builds the first modern submarine
1900	Enrico Forlanini	Builds the first hydrofoil boat
1901	The Werner brothers	Build the first modern motorcycle
1902	Henry Ford	Produces the first mass-produced cars
1903	Orville and Wilbur Wright	Make the first successful powered flight
1907	Paul Cornu	Makes the first helicopter flight
1909	Louis Blériot	Flies across the English Channel
1919	John Alcock and Arthur Brown	Fly across the Atlantic Ocean
1923	Juan de la Cierva	Builds an autogiro
1926	Robert Goddard	Builds a liquid-fuelled rocket
1936	Heinrich Focke	Builds the first successful helicopter
1937	Frank Whittle	Builds first jet engine
1939	Igor Sikorsky	Improves the helicopter
1939	Hans von Ohain	Builds the first jet aircraft that flies
1947	Charles Yeager	Makes the first faster-than-sound flight
1949		The first jet airliner, Comet, flies
1955	Christopher Cockerell	Invents the hovercraft
1961	Yuri Gagarin	The first person in space
1969	Neil Armstrong	The first person on the moon
1987	The Japanese	Try out the first train to use magnets
1988	Kanellos Kanellopoulos	Makes a record-breaking human-powered flight
1990		Solar-powered cars race in Australia

Glossary

air pollution: harmful gases in the air, caused by car exhausts or factories

autogiro: a type of aircraft with wings and propeller as well as blades like a helicopter

axle: a shaft or rod around which a wheel turns

biology: the study of living things

biologist: a scientist who studies living things

carriage: a vehicle pulled by horses

chemist: a person who studies chemistry

chemistry: the science that studies what substances are made of, how they react together, and what properties they have

combustion chamber: the part of an engine in which fuels are burned

compressed air: air that has been squeezed until it is under great pressure. It tries to expand, and this force can provide the power to run machines

compressor: a set of spinning blades in a jet engine. It squeezes air coming into the engine and forces it under pressure into the combustion chamber

commuter: a person who travels between his or her home and place of work

condense: to make a gas to change into a liquid. You condense steam into water

conveyor belt: a band or chain that moves along over a series of wheels. It carries goods through a factory

dense: heavy. Cold air is denser than hot air

dugout: a simple boat made by hollowing out a log or tree trunk

engine: a machine that converts heat energy into movement. A steam engine uses the heat of steam to drive a locomotive

experiment: a test carried out in controlled conditions to discover something new, or to prove that an idea is correct

fuel: a substance that is burnt to produce heat or power. Petrol and coal are fuels

glider: a heavier-than-air flying machine that has no engine. Gliders rely on the winds and air currents to stay in the air

helicopter: a kind of aircraft that can rise vertically from the ground, hover and move in any direction. It uses large, rotating blades to lift and move itself

hovercraft: a propeller-driven vehicle that moves on a cushion of air. Hovercraft can travel over land or sea

hull: the frame or main body of a ship

hydrofoil: a type of boat with underwater 'foil' or wings. When it reaches a certain speed, the hull rises out of the water

internal-combustion engine: a fuel-burning engine, as used in most motor vehicles. In the petrol engine, petrol vapour is burnt inside a cylinder. The gases produced expand, driving a piston down the cylinder, producing power

jet engine: a type of gas-turbine engine used in most large aircraft. A stream of hot gas is expelled from the rear of the engine, driving the aircraft forwards

locomotive: the part of a train that pushes or pulls the carriages or wagons. It contains the engine

longship: a type of ship used by the Vikings. It was long and narrow, with many oars

magnetic levitation: a way of making objects float in the air using magnets. Magnetic levitation, also called 'maglev', is used in some high-speed railway systems

mass production: a method of manufacturing in which large numbers of cars or other things are made, usually by machines

navigation: the science of directing the course of a ship or aircraft

nuclear-powered: with engines that run on energy generated by nuclear fuel

orbit: the path of a planet or other object as it moves around a planet or star in space

paddle wheel: a wheel with flat plates around its rim. The paddle wheel is attached to the back or sides of a boat and it can drive the boat backwards or forwards

physics: the science that studies matter, the forces of nature and the different forms of energy, such as heat, light and motion

physicist: a person who studies physics

piston: a circular disc that moves inside a tightly fitting cylinder, inside an engine

propeller: a device that turns very rapidly in order to pull an aircraft through the air or a ship through the water. It consists of two or more twisted blades fixed to a central shaft

robot probe: a machine that explores the surface of other planets. It is controlled from Earth

rocket: an engine driven by a stream of hot gases flowing through a nozzle at the back

rotor: a set of spinning blades, like those found on a helicopter

rudder: a broad piece of wood or metal attached to the back of a boat or ship to help steer it

science: the study of the way the world works, by using experiments and careful observation

shaft: a metal bar or rod that joins two parts of an engine

skirt: a strip of material surrounding the base of a hovercraft. It contains the air so that it forms a cushion

solar cell: a small device that turns sunlight into electricity

solar power: power that comes from sunlight and is used for driving machinery or providing heating

spoke: a strong, thin rod or wire that connects the rim of a wheel to its axle. It strengthens the wheel without making it heavy

stage coach: a horse-driven coach used to carrry people and mail on long journeys. Each journey was divided into stages with scheduled stops to change horses

steam turbine: a turbine engine that is turned by high-pressure steam

stern: the back part of a ship or boat

sternwheeler: a steam boat with a paddle wheel at the back, or stern

submarine: a vessel that travels under the sea

technology: the way the discoveries of science are used to make machines

turbine: a set of spinning blades fitted to a central shaft. The blades may be turned by gas, steam or liquid. Turbines are used in many kinds of engines and to generate electricity

vacuum: a space from which all gases or other substances have been removed

Index